SNOOPY STARS

AS

THE FITNESS FREAK

Charles M. Schulz

RAVETTE BOOKS

First published by
Ravette Books Limited 1989

Printed and bound in Great Britain
for Ravette Books Limited,
3 Glenside Estate, Star Road, Partridge Green,
Horsham, West Sussex RH13 8RA
by Cox & Wyman Ltd, Reading

ISBN 1 85304 145 9

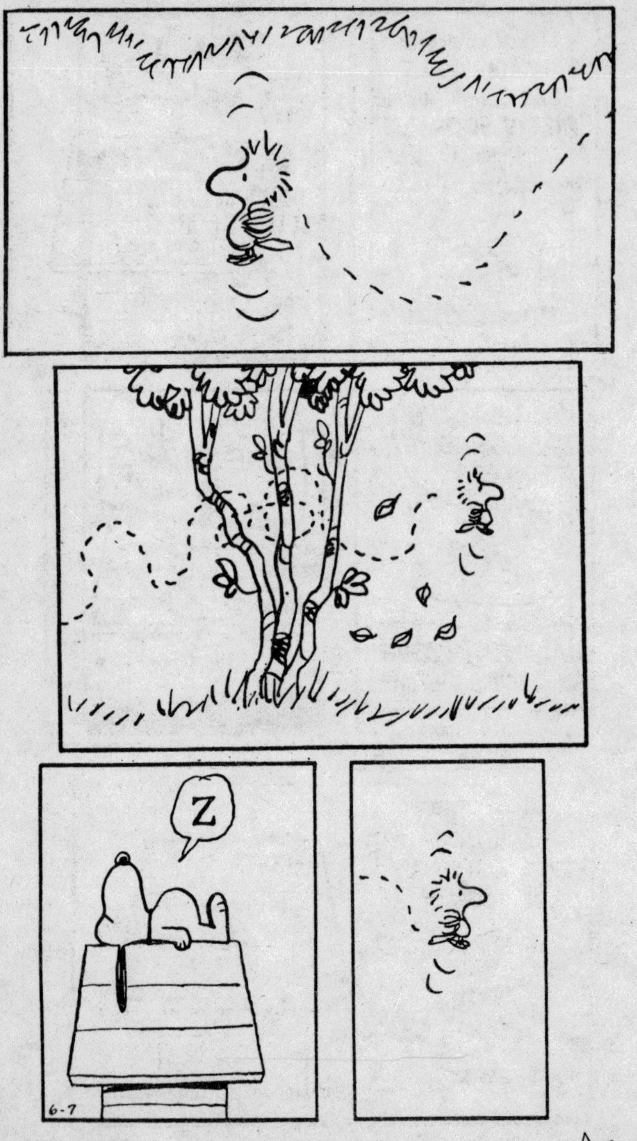
Z
6-7

7-19

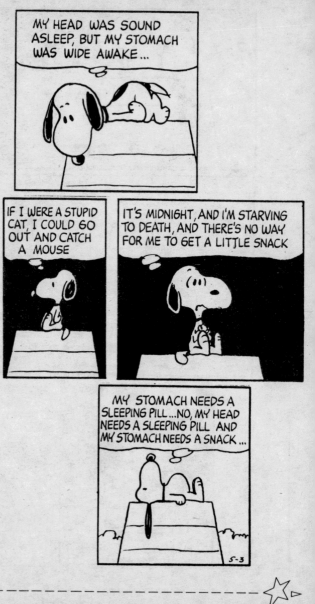

NOW, HOW IN THE WORLD DID HE KNOW I WAS HUNGRY?

WHO CAN SLEEP WITH ALL THAT MUMBLING GOING ON?

© 1978 United Feature Syndicate, Inc.

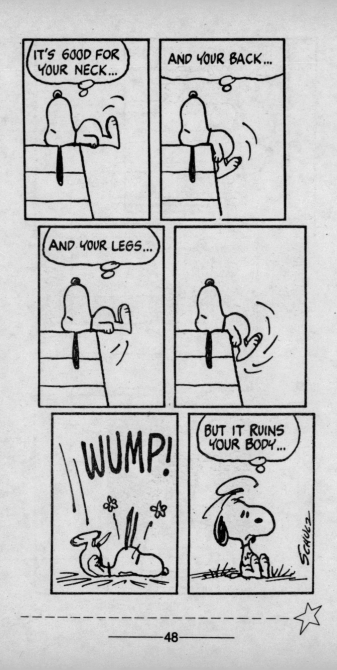

PEANUTS

GOOD GRIEF! WHAT HAPPENED TO YOU?

2-24

WELL, THERE WERE THESE THREE AIRLINE STEWARDESSES, SEE, AND THEY WERE ON RUNAWAY HORSES, SEE, AND I HAD TO SAVE THEM...

I HEARD YOU TRIPPED OVER YOUR SUPPER DISH...

AS SOON AS I GET MY CRUTCHES, I'M GOING TO START HITTING PEOPLE!

SCHULZ

I SHOULD THINK YOU'D DO BETTER IF YOU JOGGED ALONG THE SIDE OF THE ROAD SOMEWHERE

THAT'S TOO DANGEROUS...

PEOPLE RUN OUT AND BITE ME!

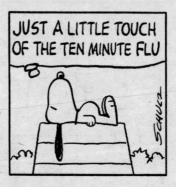

WHAT DO YOU CALL THAT?

AEROBIC SLEEPING!

I'M A NOSE, AND I'VE NEVER BEEN TO A GRINDSTONE
SO? I'M AN EAR, AND I'VE NEVER BEEN TO THE GROUND...

I'M A TAIL, AND I'VE NEVER WAGGED A DOG

Other Snoopy titles published by Ravette Books

Snoopy Stars in this series

No. 1	Snoopy Stars as The Flying Ace	£1.95
No. 2	Snoopy Stars as The Matchmaker	£1.95
No. 3	Snoopy Stars as The Terror of the Ice	£1.95
No. 4	Snoopy Stars as The Legal Beagle	£1.95
No. 5	Snoopy Stars as The Fearless Leader	£1.95
No. 6	Snoopy Stars as Man's Best Friend	£1.95
No. 7	Snoopy Stars as The Sportsman	£1.95
No. 8	Snoopy Stars as The Scourge of The Fairways	£1.95
No. 9	Snoopy Stars as The Branch Manager	£1.95
No. 10	Snoopy Stars as The Literacy Ace	£1.95
No. 11	Snoopy Stars as The Great Pretender	£1.95
No. 12	Snoopy Stars as The Dog-Dish Gourmet	£1.95
No. 14	Snoopy Stars in The Pursuit of Pleasure	£1.95
No. 15	Snoopy Stars as The Weatherman	£1.95

Colour landscapes

First Serve	£2.95
Be Prepared	£2.95
Stay Cool	£2.95
Shall We Dance?	£2.95
Let's Go	£2.95
Come Fly With Me	£2.95
Are Magic	£2.95
Hit The Headlines	£2.95

Weekenders

No. 1 Weekender	£4.95

Black and white landscapes

It's a Dog's Life	£2.50
Roundup	£2.50
Freewheelin'	£2.50
Joe Cool	£2.50
Chariots For Hire	£2.50
Dogs Don't Eat Dessert	£2.50
You're on the Wrong Foot Again, Charlie Brown	£2.50
By Supper Possessed	£2.95

All these books are available at your local bookshop or newsagent, or can be ordered direct from the publisher. Just tick the titles you require and fill in the form below. Prices and availability subject to change without notice.

Ravette Books Limited, 3 Glenside Estate, Star Road, Partridge Green, Horsham, West Sussex RH13 8RA

Please send a cheque or postal order, and allow the following for postage and packing. UK: Pocket-books – 45p for one book, 20p for the second book and 15p for each additional book. Other titles – 50p for one book and 30p for each additional book.

Name ....

Address ....

....